An Armory of Love Poems

Antavia Mason

ISBN: 978-0-578-76695-9

To my mother, the woman who always taught me that love isn't a weakness, but the very thing with which to arm myself with. You helped me realize how love truly is the greatest gift of all.

Author's Note

One of humanity's greatest longings is love. Life becomes this quest to find it, be it—to capture it between our palms like fireflies for later inspection. I write love poems because it is the one thing I find myself longing for most. This looming desire burgeoning within me to have love, give it, and harness enough of it, multiplying the magic of it all so someone who has never felt the warmth of it can learn to cozy by its fire and find rest from all the moments absent of love. When I share the story of my life and all of the moments intermingled within the folds of time, I often describe my life as one wrapped up in a theme of love. Love has always intrigued me. This feeling of never fully obtaining it and yet longing for it in ways I came to understand much more when I met God a second time when I was 16. This four-letter word captivates and seemingly evades humanity simultaneously. We are beings yearning for love, searching for it, and most times coming up short. I decided to embark on this journey of releasing these poems because love comes to us in different stages, different places, and people. Love is a powerful motivator, and when we learn to accept love, it becomes easier to give it—which is something our world needs. Pockets of our reality exist starved of love, souls, starved for love. With these poems, I hope you sense glimpses of love in its many forms. Taking with you the truth of how love encapsulates this human experience, this cosmically beautiful existence that is nothing short of a miracle.

On most days I arm myself with love poems
because I feel that is all it would take to
conquer the hours before me

Contents

I

III

Acknowledgments

I

Summer 2017, First Impressions

I remember the first time we met,
we shook hands and you exchanged a small smile
for my extraordinarily large one and your eyes followed
my bouncing frame of excitement and measured my words as each syllable flowed
like waterfalls over cliffs, and your eyes sparkled just slightly

you were either amazed at my ability to speak so fast and I
asked you questions times infinity that ranged just above superficiality

every moment after that was filled with a quiet observance on your part
and a nosy intrigue on mine, my questions remained constant while
your answers leaked out ever so slightly,
filling my desire to know you little by little

the day we found a commonality I remember the light in your eyes
and the rhythm of our bodies swaying to the tempo of salsa on
an aged piano and after we'd finished swaying, hips matching the
leading of feet, I remember walking away feeling magic in my bones
not wanting the dance to end

Easy to Love

To think of you is to ruminate
on endless possibilities of a perhaps
we may never fully know

A Short Poem to Mary Oliver

You taught me to write love poems to trees
to fall in love with how they sway, to remember their
dance on nights filled with spring and
you whispered of love, so sacred and so pure,
of how hands can form unions bold enough to last
and how sorrow, although burdensome will
almost always give way to light

A Ferris Wheel Kind of Person

I am a Ferris wheel kind of person
I like to circle things, going around
one possibility, hanging on for the next ride,
I am the child who does not want to leave the top
instead I want to hog the space
just beneath stars and their moon
smiling at those below who have not gotten
the chance to see this view

I am a hold-my-seat-the-ride-can-still-go-on kind of person
I am not fond of letting go because
every moment has the opportunity to be better
than its last second
and this Ferris wheel kind of person
likes to take things slow, going around
at a pace leaving me the chance to take it all in,
laughter from below where couples first begin,
catching glimpses of hands first held
and smiles so large the wind catches on
to the corners of their joy

To Linger in an Aisle of Books with You

If you were mine, I'd like to start over
I would like the chance to
stand by you on that aisle of books in a local Walmart
thumbing through pages of our perhaps
and choose to turn every page with anticipation
that this story would end the way I want it to

If you were mine, time would slow down,
infinity would only be the beginning
and all the moments I missed would
be chances offered again and
I would cherish every single one

Centerpiece

this place,
ebbing the way
silence does, making
its way into peace

this place
used to feel empty
like insides stripped away
making its way into brokenness

now this place feels like
healing, pieces ebbing
and floating onto a table of thanksgiving

I am the centerpiece,
my soul a display
of placing not-so-together
things into a formation of hope

a cornucopia of mending,
this is fruitfulness--a lesson
on how to stitch and sew memories
of pain into a quilt of giving

I am giving,
lending out love
without expectation

this place, this soul, this love
I've learned to accept,
to take what's been given,
wrap it into gifts of forgiveness

sharing these intricately wrapped
boxes for unsuspecting receivers
hoping they accept what took me
so long to unravel

Trust

It lingers on your words
reassuring me that this life I
live has a place within purpose
although some moments seem to
outweigh the beauty of grace
my heart lingers on your
breath, your words, your hope
becoming my hope

Our Hearts are Red Balloons

I like to believe that when
balloons free fall in an upward motion,
love, like helium takes them to this place

where like red balloons we dance
within the sphere of clouds
unafraid of this height

the distance will not frighten us
we, used to taking risks
with these emotions

hoping this time
the flight will be one that lasts,
the sun our beaming example

of how passion may dim,
yet the flames can still burn
and when night falls
we become kindling
dancing behind curtains of stars

Patience

Let me be patient

Let my heart learn
the t e m p o of waiting

so, when the day comes
I will understand all the more
why you were worth the

w a i t

01 March 2018, I Hope This Poem Finds You Well

A thousand conversations never to be had
we rest silently on words wrapped in similes
covered in poetry

our lips, thin lines of heartbeats ready to dance upon
pulses we can only make together, like strings
and melodies make compositions inspired by lovers,
the ones who take art, holding it in the palms of their
hands like stars too bright for darkness to dim

we miss movements as feet dance lightly on
affection tinged with intrigue and our arms lock
to rhythm and hips sway to beats that drum
out the music of souls too in sync to be off kilter

Before We Fall

sips of tea
warm as the sun on
flower-scented smiles
gleaming in the satisfying
moments of hands first held
underneath stars and moon
awaiting love to bloom

Beginning

What today holds
lingers behind eyelids
heavy with yesterday's moments
learning how to open wholly to
see the sun yet again, gazing at
the rise of its shape as if it is the
very first time irises have beheld light
like fire, yellow like the burning of all
the things that didn't make sense, yet now,
underneath the glow of its beauty, warmth
feels familiar and light feels like the beginning
of everything we used to yearn for

Days Pass Too Quick

Days pass
Too quick to count
And the distance
Between us lessens
The way a balloon
Releases warm air
From puckered lips
Brushing, grazing
Against a lover's
In the expectancy
That it won't be
The last time

Our Two Hearts

lie with me here
in fading sunlight,
just as the stars break through
into night and my head will
find comfort nestled in the space
between your neck and shoulder
as arms enfold me like safety
and smiles become softer
here in the warmth of
our two hearts
melding into one
bidding the moon
goodnight

One Day in Winter

wintry winds gliding on
the light of moon-soaked
stars, a place where quiet
reverberates off the skin
of bare trees and the
chill of night feels like
home and the tender kisses
of snowflakes against
smiling eyes the shape of
hope brings to the forefront
all the things wished
for in last winter's
snow

There Were Lighthouse in His Eyes

you have left me wishing for more
for more moments in time
where you sat with me
silently in a room, the atmosphere
filled with the weight of your eyes
brown, but speckled with sunlight
leaving streaks of stars in their wake

the last time we spoke
your words were miniscule
meters, phrases on poetry,
on class schedules and summer plans
I wished to be a part of

yet, I still remember your eyes
inquisitive lighthouses beaming
to me questions I could not answer
because I did not know how to take
all of you in, you,
a frame of brilliant light
I find myself wishing for all the time

What Flowers Can Teach Us

flowers need not lessons on how to bloom,
it is in their very nature to grow into
the very thing they were created to be

our humanity was created to bloom,
to bridge together pieces of our souls
etching them into the fabric of sunlight
making room for grace the way petals
open themselves up to wind and warmth

we were made for blooming,
made for sun-kissed smiles drenched
in the rain of hearts learning how to
dance in unity

we were made to bathe in the hopes
of our tomorrows and learn from the
sorrows of our yesterdays

like flowers in fields learning
what communion feels like,
we are sunflowers tethered by our stems
all reaching for the light

may we always know that
sunlight is meant for us

meant for our bodies to know
the warmth of its embrace
to know the curvature of the sun's smile

may we remember that
sunlight and fields speak to the joy
of where we belong

A Scale of Infinity

All we have is time
so let us rest with in the folds
of passing minutes
your eyes keeping track of time
on a scale of infinity
as I rest my head on
your ticking heart
content in a moment
of perfect tranquility
while your kisses, short
like flashing seconds
become all I'm waiting for

Some Days After Winter

I remember the month of your birthday
although we've never celebrated one together
I remember the smallness of our conversations,
how they always fell short and seemed to linger
at the same time

My memory is full of you, running images
of timid glances and stoic gazes, those times etched
into me because I will them so, and now I question
if letting them go will somehow bring you back to me,
memories riding on the wind like the petals of dandelions
in the hopes this prayer will come true

Thoughts in Orbit

It isn't as if
it's all supposed to make sense
how my thoughts are all their own
and each one seems to revolve around you

today you are the sun and the moon,
the reason love has learned to orbit the
perimeter of my smile

An Emily Dickinson Kind of Hope

Hope is the thing
with feathers,
taking flight within
the walls of my heart

she flutters next to this
pulsing symphony,
wings flapping against
cacophonous rhythm

I almost wish for
her to take flight

To Be a Garden Brimming

This love is weighted
it carries the force of the wind
and the height of the sun.

Like trees grounded in soil
your love is mine
strong and rooted
within the folds of my heart.

You have made a garden here
my being made of blooming
where darkness finds no home
because here, we are flowers,
magnolias abiding in the core of love
always brimming with spring

The Kiss of Sunlight

a kiss of sunlight
just below the lobe of the ear
bringing warmth to skin
once cold
here, longing
coalesces into peace
this feeling lingers

Coffee Smiles

coffee smiles and mocha kisses
on hazy Sunday evenings
where the sun sits atop expectancy
in wait of the moon for relief
and we lie entangled in its warmth
blankets forsaken and arms
the only covering we need

How Will We Be Good?

How will we be good?
you, all smiles and brown eyes
that match the rays of the sun

&

me, the lover with expectations
the height of the heavens
and a heart wanting to be cherished
How will we be good?

Distance

Times waits for no man
nor woman strong enough
to lasso the seconds and light years
racing between time and space
to bring one closer to another

An Invitation

I didn't give you a chance,
not one opportunity to prove my indifference
weak-willed, my declines as apprehension
because I couldn't believe what you
truly wanted was me

I took your glances for granted,
your miniscule smiles and how
every tentative step you took
towards me beckoned a simple reply,
you were a pursuer looking for
a yes in non-verbal cues
I didn't realize you wanted

Wonderland

I wonder to myself about you
I allow my mind to wander off into
rabbit holes shrouded in mystery
and sometimes one thought
finds another, they continue in adventure,
wrap themselves around possibilities
and hope to find Wonderland

Museums of Anticipation

we are the definition of strangers
I know not of who you are
what you like, what you love

you know not of what makes me smile
or what makes me laugh
your voice has not yet met my ears
your eyes, haven't the pleasure of gracing
me with the sweetest gift of seeing into your soul

we are the definition of unknown
you are a book I have yet to read,
poems I have yet feel in my bones,
art I am eager to gaze upon

we are the definition of anticipation
an ellipsis of sorts, hanging in
the balance for the next of all the
words we've prepared within the caverns
of our beings, learning how to read the stars
that will lead us to each other

The Upside of Valleys

Valleys are just inverted mountains,
when life proved too hard for the rockiness
of their frames they caved in on themselves

these strong bold things afraid of not being strong enough,
yet not realizing how deep love goes down beneath the earth
to make stone and rock and dirt rise to the sky like hope
with wings large enough to rest near the glow of the sun

we can learn from these mountains,
the way they fit themselves into the grooves of earth for survival,
although our frames may not tower the way theirs do
we swell, looming with love resting near the space of heaven

Roots

we are roots learning
how to embrace on cold nights,
I practice weaving into you
acclimating myself to your shape

you, holding the limbs of my soul
I am still learning how to water
as we burrow deep into the earth
using soil as a foundation for beauty,
intertwined in darkness
prepping for the light

The Arrival of Finally

When time closes its gap
I hope in that moment
there will be grace for my brokenness
and joy for the sorrow that will be shed

When the seconds slow to ticking
and breathing becomes even

I know in those moments
only you and I will exist
as time continues to spin and
stars resume their twinkling dance
against the sky reminding us how
beauty is forged in darkness

Where Does the Waiting End?

Where does the waiting end in a world
where hearts are clocks set for morning
only to be met with the quiet of night?

When does love arrive?

I wonder what she will look like and will
I know how to greet her when she comes

Will she surprise me
appearing when the sun
has just awakened or
will she be as silent as a
shooting star?

bright and purposeful against
what we see as unending

Will she rest in your smile?

her feet moving to the rhythm
your heart makes, a sound
I hope to grow familiar to

Let Us Make Room for Eternity

In a sacred pocket of space sometime
in the future, we will be together
The memory of the distance we once felt
so strongly will be wiped from the present
because there will only be us

Time, a friend we loathed, we now cherish
for the minutes we hold are seconds far too
beautiful to count on imbalanced hands.

Instead, our fingers will count breaths and laughs
as eyes take in small smiles, and sun-glinted skin,
here, time finally making room for eternity

Longing

like deep inhales
before sky-deep plunges
into an unknown

I have not known
this feeling
bold and pure
that rests between a
space fully soul and heart

The Tides of Memory

falling in love is a skill to master
to train my ears in the ways of your
laughter so that my heart knows when to beat
to teach my eyes the art of gazing
for when your smile is the only thing
I want to remember

These Times

These times
trying and hard like
the blues songs my grandmother
used to listen to seep into questions

What kind of lover will I be,
to you, the one whose love
feels taxing and strange,
burning like whiskey down
my virgin throat

this sensation reeks of a hope
I forced myself to no longer feel

What kind of love can you give
to me, worn and weary yet
longing and craving for this
in the warmth of a soul
you seem to have rekindled

What kind of love can
we form, the curvatures of
our spines leaning in for
caresses of support

In these trying times
I'm choosing you as
a lover, as a friend

your arms, your lips, this space.
For these trying times
will you choose me too

II

Circa 2013

Circa 2013 I found friends,
we developed a kinship over Chick-Fil-A lemonade
and shared a large appreciation
for authors we dream of
becoming one day

We have albums of laughter,
Polaroid photos of time framed
upon the walls of our hearts and minds

These friends, long lasting pieces
of a puzzle I grew tired of
forcing into wholeness

Now, it is kindred and beautiful
and when we need reminders
we grapple towards the memories
of our younger selves, smaller versions
of our adulthood still forming

For Emma Lou, Spring on Your Porch

spring days,
faintly hinting of Mississippi summers,
tickling grass sprouting
between toes wriggling in glee and sunlit warmth

bodies on porches emitting noontime laughter
and gleaming smiles
your frame, a filling vision of joy
and a smile like sun
wide and bright

A Palm Full of Stars

As a child my hands were small enough
to palm stars from the sky,
my eyes wide enough to hold light
like sun, unafraid of darkness.
Heartbeats were frequent like the flashing
of fireflies on summer evenings
and in the covering of night between the
speckles of light, I would pray
that love would arrive one of these days
like a prince on a stallion and I would then
know the truth of fairytales

Younger

younger,
wiser and unaware
of a world much bigger than me
small and gentle like wind
on worn petals

young,
like the budding of
growth ripe with anticipation
to be taller than trees
arms reaching into
clouds of limitless hope

Breath, A Hard Thing to Catch

I have fallen in like before
experienced the inevitable flight of
butterflies between the space
of my heart and lungs making
breath a hard thing to catch

A Love in this Life and the Next

When the time comes
    I hope to be everything
prayed for in the tender moments
    of longing

when time ceases to move in the
    way it tends to do when souls align
in this life and the next

I hope to find solace in your
    laughter, my heart making a
home in the sound of you

Gemela

we were strength from the very beginning
born of each other, my half supplementing yours
in utter seclusion below starry skies where hazy
humid nights beckoned the arrival of summer

Sister,
Formed to fit the places in need of sunlight
when Mississippi scorching burned too bright
on the backs of our innocence

My sister,
I will always remember those summers with you
the flowers I picked for my hair, a crown of
rainbows after the rain
you and laughter, running
barefoot in pastures of our own wonder

Bloom Past the Withering

stages of growth
measured in the height of a sunflower
a stance reaching sky and warmth

she, rooted under what
cannot bury experience,
an elevated strength
in the width of stems

green like grass that
has learned to bloom
past the withering

Lessons for Moving On

when it all passed
I forgot how to cherish
the small things.
I held onto the pain of
yesterdays the way thorns
hope to never release the innocent from
thickets of curiosity.
It all became a blur, a

m

a

z

e

a puzzle of pieces never
fitting until I learned how to
let go of the unforgivable and love
what seemed unlovable

fireflies

fireflies are full of life
their flickering signifying
subtle vitality, strength
in each beat of luminescent breath.

I'd like to be a firefly
used to a slow and steady flight
learning to light my path
an inch at a time
edging along centimeters
aware of how short living can be
yet how large love looms in light
of my frailness

I wouldn't waver at uncertainty
I would fly towards wonder
flap my wings at her whimsy
marveling at how even in the
thickening night
I am still full of life

This Universe Has Space for Me

parts of me I find dwelling in ethers of time
waiting for a big bang, a creation of sorts
these parts are halves and wholes,
lopsided musings.
I take time remembering their shapes
and their curves, a geometric sensuality

pieces of me averse to the rigidity of linearity
straight edges giving only two directions—
forward or backward.
most moments I veer off to the sides
finding something else, anything else

like pockets of possibilities that can jettison me
off into the night sky beaming to a million
tiny stars—this is how I want to live

my parts and pieces, halves and wholes abiding in light
speckled within dusk, luminescent crescents of fire
burning too bright to fully gaze upon

I will be dwelling—spread like hope and sun and moon,
there are thousands of me, effulgent
reflections of life

Octaves of Kinship

family, the syllables stretch
like foreign octaves in the grooves
of my throat, scratching
to come forward
reaching my tongue,
the taste all too familiar
yet, mildly complex
against the simplicity of my desire
to extend beyond the need of other

family, multi-layered and
full of joy, learning how to extricate
from pain making headway to laughter
to hope, to beyond where needing others
is second nature and we build upon the layers
of our laughter creating legacies of peace

we are fit for this journey,
excavators of the past,
these stories making music,
a crescendo

Raindrops & Loneliness

in all that loneliness brings
it has never brought
you to me the way rain
brings with it all of itself
barreling, hurdling to the ground
in all its weightless glory knowing
in its tiny form gravity serves
as fate and the ground is
another lover deep and profound
ready to accept this little
raindrop for all that it is

The Curve of a Heartbeat

Remember,

love is not him
passion and intimacy are not forsaken in
the way he used to smile at you
because the fire you yearn for did not
lie in the sparkle of his eyes
even if they used to sparkle for you

Remember,

it is okay to mourn this loss
hope will find its way back to you,
cradle its body against the curve of your heartbeat
and love will not be far behind
because sometimes it takes losing the fire
to know why it burns in the first place

A

Reprieve

of

Haikus

Delicate

You are delicate,
pieces of you found amongst
leaves scattered in fall

Making Stars Our Freedom

I find us in space
we making stars our freedom
peace found in the night

Floating Irises

Floating irises
vision clearer than before,
a future of us

Beneath Weeping Willows

these days remind me of quieter times
simpler moments draped in the
sun of Autumnal graces and freedom
feels like wind beneath all the things
thought impossible

here, peace finds me below weeping
willows, my back supported by the strength
of nature's own pain, leaves and vines free
falling between the world and my worn frame,
a drapery of warmth against the chill
of all my yesterdays

A Series of Perhaps

I

A perhaps is all we need
we'll find it underneath tree leaves
covered lightly in fall, and
we'll use our fingers to brush away
the dust of yesterday and as
we raise yellow and red to hazy orange
we'll find the beauty for which we started
the search

II

I remember how he made me want to feel
how the existence of him evoked a desire purely wholesome
in that I simply wanted to be the center of his affection,
a singular point on the curve of every question asked of love,
and when his eyes roved over silent questions
in quiet conversation, I wanted to feel the brown
of his irises making contact with mine,
both of us understanding that perhaps,
we could fit together

The Moon's Craters

I remember the light in his eyes
the very first time we met.
That was the day I told my heart
to be cautious, to beware of
lilting smiles and sun-filled eyes,
because even though he shimmered
and his stares warmed
parts of me I'd never shown the sun
I knew eventually
the sun would set

When night came
and the moon decided to shine,
I found myself unprepared for the
darkness, his eyes now
craters floating in space no longer
tinged with starlight,
it was here I forgot what warmth
felt like

Breath

I made you my next breath
my inhales like medicine mending
an ailment of a broken heart
yet, when I'm not with you
I find that breathing is all the
more easier

the way my lungs
have learned to love the taste of air
my mouth, growing accustomed to
the familiarity of its curving,
this next breath

it feels like living

WINDOWS

windows, my steeple reaching
out and up towards sky
the clouds, faint glances of heaven
mirroring the whispers of love
sometimes hidden in the rain
of evening

The Monsoon

I didn't get my license until I was 23
I remember the day, how the clouds
danced overhead into shadows and
my silent prayers that these clouds
would hold the rain within themselves,
showing enough restraint until after
the driving test

To ask of someone to hold something
within themselves that they must let go of
is never wrought in kindness,
yet I persisted with this prayer
lifting from my lips in small whispers hoping
they'd reach heaven, the place just above the
space where rain dwelled

I met you when I was 22,
I remember the day, how sweltering
the sun felt, and how when I looked
up at you, your smile held whimsy
and a laughter, I seemed to pull
out of you easily
I never asked you to hold
anything in.

To ask of someone to give you
something they do not contain
within themselves is never
wrought in selfishness
yet, I persisted in asking,
in hoping my silent prayers
would be enough to keep you
to myself just above the space
of my lungs close enough to
cradle you to my heart

When the rain fell
I remembered the prayers
I prayed for you, how my tears
warped into pellets dropping

from the sky like bombs,
it was not enough to keep you

To ask of someone to be
the answer to everything
may be too much to ask

I realize now how my
questions were too big at the time
my clouds too heavy for your heart
my sun, beaming too loud
for your shadows

In Being Alone

In being alone,
I find reprieve from the expectation of romance
I fancy myself a woman patient, yet willing,
a structure of confidence adorned in moments
of wondering when the time will be right,
yearning for the stars to align in poetic rhythm
and beam us toward one another

but for now,
I am content to be the moon
suspended in solitude
cradling the craters of my own love,
learning to nurture the parts of me
I've yet to discover

The Distance Light Can Travel

This
is
all
we
ever
were

silent stars that burned in the darkness
passion forged in solitude
never reaching, never touching
only existing light years apart

Today We Made Healing

today we made light within the pain
laughed at foolishness and
the whimsy of sorrow
finding joy amidst the turmoil

today we made healing,
fashioned it from ourselves
attached it to sunlight
holding it far from our view
to catch a better glimpse

Reflections, May 25th

Yesterday I turned 25,
and the sun rose behind the clouds
shielding the light but for a moment.
I don't know what these numbers hold
nor how the moments of my yesterday
and today will converge into tomorrows.
I do know what hope feels like,
I know how joy tastes after 25 years
of not knowing.
I see how laughter
is sweeter here in this year and
find that my heart still knows
how to wait for the right kind
of love where flowers and their
petals are always rising to the sun
even on the days it chooses
to bloom behind the clouds

III

All Too Beautiful

The wind lingers on the soft whisper of your lips
I am drawn by the sway of your song and the force of your dance
This moment is magic and in this second I am captivated by you,
stilled by the strength of your beauty
and the smile of your heart.
This is you and I can finally accept it.
This is us and now I know that this
was all I ever wanted from you,
to know that your love compares to none and
the weight of your heart carrying mine is all the
help I will ever need in the storms of life,
because your strength is all encompassing and all powerful.
You are the sun to my darkest nights, the wind to my rustling heart
and the rain to the drought of my soul
You are metaphors I cannot breathe out fast enough,
poetry I cannot drive my fingers to write
You are similes I dare not force my ink to spill
because you are all too beautiful
to capture in the lines of rhyme and meter,
all too lovely to suspend on paper.

Last Night We Made Tea

Last night we made tea
I poured water into an aged tea kettle
and watched you grab tea from the cupboard
a few inches above me, my smile
caught your eye and as we waited for water to
boil and the kettle's high, shrill song
you leaned in for a kiss, soft and sweet
and for a moment I forgot the water
simmering to a boil and the steaming mist
rising to a whistle

This is How God Loves You

This is how God loves you,
He has made stars your pathway
so that when darkness tries its best
there is a twinkling reminder of grace.
He has made flowers for blooming,
a beauty built upon vibrancy
so when your past rears strong
His grace abounds

Measures of Wholeness

Love as if the wind will not move unless
your heart creates the rhythm
sing songs of heartbreak and turn them
into melodies of passion
Sweet one, write poems and let each
line of meter and string of similes spark
the healing you need

A Moondance of Sorts

I sleep with the shades to my window open
at night when the moon is on full display,
my room lights up with silver and on
especially cloudy nights the moon dances
in between the shadows casting a sort
of moonlit dance onto the ballroom of my wall

I lie in stillness and watch this waltz,
the window my own makeshift skylight
lifting me to the moon and her craters,
this is the kind of darkness I am not afraid of,
this feels like magic and resilience

I never knew shrouded in night,
the moon and the clouds
could be this beautiful

Beside Stillness

at the end of it all
I want to rest beside your stillness,
for you to calm the raging storm
that quakes within my bones,
to lie in the quiet space of your warmth
and know that in our realm of existence
you are pleased with the way I've lived
in view of you

We Hold Symphonies in Our Gaze

Goodness resides here
a kind of warmth
that makes music with the sun
and when your eyes meet mine
I see stars align in the sphere
of your irises

We are two different rhythms
trying to create a sound
reminiscent of heaven,
angelic choruses
joining in on this symphony

From Whom All Blessings Flow

To the Lover of my soul
from whom all blessings flow,
You are the sum of all good things
sunshine, bright and capable of warming
all that dares intimacy with winter,
you are spring within budding flowers,
droplets of rain tattooed to
petals that find themselves
open to the sky awaiting more

What It Means to Miss Someone

Yesterday, when the rain fell
droplets hung onto windowpanes
and looked for the sun just beyond
the clouds and grace found us there
waving to the sky like long-lost
friends who forgot what missing
people and places felt like

Nature's Internal Metronome

The next moment is unknown
expectancy lies in wait for
its chance to arrive,
for the sun to rise, breaking through
sleepy Dawn's colors with
pulsing yellows and baby blues

She is waiting for noon, for
that stand still moment
in time where day slows
down to earth's internal metronome

Moments in Waiting

Rest makes space for the uneasiness
in my soul to wither away
he calls to me to find quiet
and creates solace in the midst
of my own thoughts

I am a lady in waiting, riding on the arms
of clocks elongating the meeting of us

The Stars Have Influence

The stars have influence upon
the way I choose to love you,
when you are light years away
I still gaze upon the way you shine
miles away in the twilight sky,
the way you warm my coldest nights
and the way your light always
guides me home before the rising
tide of dawn

The Earth Speaks of You

earth moves alongside
the whisperings of you,
trees have learned the
rhythm of your movement
and rain falls in time to
tender reminders of healing

Cosmic Impossibilities

In my hoping
I find impossibilities
inferior to the beating
of my heart's confidence

I am hope on wings
untethered by physics
I am an anomaly in the
face of the mosaic of
my own doubt

it isn't strong enough,
these fragments of unbelief
to swallow up the waves
of my faith that somewhere
across the cosmic course of my life
love is choosing to find its way
to me

For Wonder

in wonder we find
the parts of ourselves
left behind in winter's bloom,
snowcapped memories buried
beneath frost-bitten kisses

here, we find warmth
a place where extremities
make way for limberness
tinged and graced by Joy's fire

we have discovered why nature's
song belts with ease like an Autumn
wind carrying yesterday's weight
like a tornado funneling the bodies
of lifeless foliage full of yellows and oranges

here, wonder is old friend
full of fond memories,
he makes smiling easy
and good things better than
we hoped them to be

The Light of a Thousand Suns

When we are together
yesterday fades away like
the fog of morning and
clouds beam the loveliest
hue of moments forged with
the light of a thousand suns

I'm No Seamstress

I will not forget the hope
I used as warmth on
still winter nights

Where loneliness felt more
like a cloak of my own making
the stitching worn from my
desire to add more than needed

I'm no seamstress, not of fabric anyways
so, hope became my medium
the form taking on my being
wrapping and covering
what I could not

I will not forget the hope
I used as warmth on
still, winter nights

All Things Small and Large

all things, small and large
like sky remind me of you,
swelling clouds the color
of wholeness,

a seeking desire willing
itself to be found

things like this, like vast
blue, reminiscent of
cascading waves rushing
forward with the whoosh
of the wind carrying heaven with it,

this expanse of
all things living in a land
where joy blossoms each morning
and the sun is on a loop
perpetuating a brilliant beauty
the color of hues
we have no words for

The Walls of Our Hearts

There was time long ago
when love brought joy even in
the midst of sorrow once
felt so strongly.
A time where wind hugged
trees on Autumn days and
the sun whispered secrets to
clouds full of hope and
when warmth felt far-flung
we would use the walls of
our hearts to cover the sacred
places kept aside for each other

Where the Light Lands

If this is all there is to life
I long for the days where the sun
will shine brighter and the stars
will respond with a kiss of their own light
and we'll bathe underneath the sheen of
a moonstruck gleam, our eyes choosing
to see where the light does shine
instead of where it doesn't

In What I Cannot Change

tomorrow's apostrophes are all his own,
they, curved into belonging where yesterday
is still learning to let go.
she holds on with hope, a ferocious grip laden
with commas and ellipses yearning for time to
rewind and stand still,

yet,

tomorrow persists in the efforts to take what
belongs to him, cradling expectation with arms
the length of pathways meant for traversing
because everything begins with a journey,
a moment, an actionable thought that what
we cannot change today can always
be made better tomorrow

,

Melodies

This feels impossible
the search for you in the recognition
of irises I've never seen before
I miss you without ever knowing what
having you felt like

These days you have felt closer
than yesterday, your warmth preceding
your presence

and here I am, waiting like spring hidden
within bulbs after winter,
finding glimpses of you in the songs I
listen to and every day I
hope to find the tune we are
both singing, our feet stepping
in sync to a melody we've always
known existed

The Art of Hope

It can be a tiresome game,
learning the art of hope and
choosing to practice its beauty
at the wrong moments

yet, on most days,
I pull out the tools
displaying them before my expectation
just when I think, maybe, this time
they'll work

Belief in Love

I believe in love,
her embrace and her smile
etched between those things
I'd rather forget

I believe her to be stronger
than self, for in her I see
all the things she finds
breathtakingly beautiful

One Singular Moment

I fear hoping for the wrong things,
the wrong people, forging my future
in the smile of one person who reminds
me of sunlight and hope like ancient beauty
set aside for a great unveiling.
I fear wanting to know you more than you desire me
and at night when the moon arrives and the stars
beam into existence against the canvas of midnight
blue I wish upon every coruscating being that I could
be given one singular moment to try again.

In the Eve of Love Awakening

In the eve of love awakening
for the first time, remind me
of all the promises I made
to myself before I met you.

A time before I knew the
warmth of your eyes, the
color of an Autumn sunset,
before I knew what your
smile tasted like and how
the sweetness of your
presence held everything
within me, reassuring
me of all that I am

A Good Job at Loving You

Because I am practicing at loving myself well I
oftentimes tell God that I think
I could do a good job at loving you.
He and I find moments late into the night where
lamps beam a hazy kind of warmth
the color of September's harvest and words make space for you

Because I am learning to love myself well, my heart is
gaining momentum around laps of hope and
with each sprint grace becomes my oxygen and
daydreams fit into my reality and praying for you is
like peppermint tea before bed—warm and intentional

Because I am loving myself well as each day passes,
I hope that you are doing the same
and that sunrises glisten like beacons for you
resounding hope like Orion's brilliance
because you deserve love even if it isn't with me,
although on most days I hope it will be

Acknowledgements

Here we are, the end of a collection of poems I hope you enjoyed. These poems only exist because of the overwhelming support of friends and family who believed in my words when I, at times, doubted their validity and worth.

To my mother, thank you for allowing words to be my haven. When I told you I wanted to be a writer you didn't miss a beat. Your encouragement reverberates throughout these poems. I love you dearly, my sweet momma.

Thank you to my dearest sister, my twin—Octavia, I love how God placed us together—your creativity and love and strength uphold me. Life is better with you by my side and I am so grateful that poetry is something we share, among having shared a womb.

Thank you to my friends, Victoria Atterberry, Samantha Bruner, and Victoria Attia (my sweet Sangermano). You are the ones I never had to beg to let me read poetry aloud to you (no matter the time or place). You helped me find my voice and made our dorm room floors my first ever stage. All of the moments we've spent together writing and reading and critiquing have made me a better writer.

Thank you, Professor Keith Gogan, my very own Mr. Keating(if you haven't seen *Dead Poets Society*, I highly recommend it.). I have learned so much from you. Your poise and grace and honesty when it came to my work has been a blessing all its own. The lessons you have shared of the craft of poetry will be something I carry with me as I continue to grow as a poet and writer and human being. Thank you truly does not suffice for all that you have taught me in my short time at ORU.

Thank you to Dr. William Epperson. One who will not have the chance to know these poems this side of heaven. It was truly an honor to know the man who would recite poetry on a whim. Being in your presence evoked a spirituality of literature and prose I am still learning to cultivate.

Thank you to all of the ones I've met who sparked a notion of love within me. To the ones not named, the ones who left me stronger than I was before I met you, thank you. And for the ones I still pray for to this day, memories of you can be found lingering in these poems.

About the Author

Antavia Mason is a writer, poet, and creator. Born and raised in Meridian, Mississippi she began writing stories at a young age and developed a love for poetry. As a creator, she desires to express creativity in a way that inspires others to understand their own innate creativity. When she's not writing she can be found trying out Pinterest recipes, drinking copious amounts of tea, and steadily cultivating a daily writing habit.

Other books by Antavia Mason

For Wonder in the Wilderness

Stay Connected
penofthebeloved.com